Telegraph & Argus

Bygone Bradford

Telegraph & Argus

Bygone Bradford

Compiled by
Jim Appleby

Breedon Books
Publishing Company
Derby

First published in Great Britain by
The Breedon Books Publishing Company Limited
44 Friar Gate, Derby, DE1 1DA.
1995

ISBN 1 85983 032 3

Printed and bound by Butler & Tanner, Caxton Works, Frome, Somerset.
Covers printed by Premier Print, Nottingham.

Contents

Foreword

THE position of a newspaper in any community is one of unique privilege. To many it is a confidant: people whisper things to newspapers they wouldn't tell even their closest friends. To others, it is a catalyst 'silent majority'.

For most of its readers, however, it is the lifeblood of the local community, keeping them in touch with all that's new and different, everything that might in some way touch their lives and, often, a lot more besides.

As such, a newspaper as well-established as the *Telegraph & Argus* provides an astonishingly detailed insight into the lives of local people. The names and faces of the great and good, the ordinary and the not-so-good pass through its pages, leaving a mark on time that, for many, would otherwise go unrecorded.

The *Telegraph & Argus*, in one form or another, has been around since 1868, when it was first published as the *Bradford Daily Telegraph* – although the first newspaper in its family to appear was the *Bradford Observer* in 1834. Although much of the material gathered in those early days is lost, the *T&A's* library is stuffed with images evoking the decades that have passed since – the fashions, the trends, the life-styles of changing generations.

But more than just a social record, it also provides a fascinating window on the physical character and development of the city and its surrounding areas, from the sadly mourned architectural gems swept away in an era of harsh modernity to their under-designed concrete and glass replacements many of which, today, are already showing the patina of age.

This book is a dip into those archives. In many ways it can only scratch the surface of the history it attempts to record. But we hope the careful selection of photographs in these pages will provide a flavour of the proud past of an important city.

Hopefully, as the reader browses through, he or she can do so with the assurance that their own lives, their own community, their own era will, in some way, be leaving their impression on the pages of the *Telegraph & Argus*.

And, who knows, in some future book . . .

Perry Austin-Clarke
Editor
Telegraph & Argus
July 1995, Bradford

Acknowledgements

The bulk of the work for this book was carried out by the compiler, *Telegraph & Argus* journalist Jim Appleby, who tapped his not inconsiderable knowledge of Bradford to produce captions which we hope are both informative and entertaining. The same sort of care and thought went into his selection of photographs from the *T&A's* vast library. Thanks also go to other *T&A* staff who helped in this project, most notably Mandy Murray and Mike Priestley.

The *T&A's* news vendors have been a feature on the streets for nearly 130 years. One of the best known around Forster Square in the 1950s and 60s was Paddy Perry, seen here putting the paper to good use during a heatwave in 1960.

In Adversity
Chapter One

Masonry comes crashing down as a warehouse in Nelson Street is destroyed by fire in 1965.

After one of the worst winters on record, Bradford was also hit by floods in 1947. This was Broadway, with the Post Office on the right and City Hall in the distance.

Heavy snow trapped people in their homes at Queensbury in 1958. Spades were needed to free them.

Thousands queued outside St George's Hall, the Connaught Rooms in Mannington Lane and elsewhere for emergency smallpox vaccinations in 1962 after the disease was found in the city.

Bradford Beck, prone to flooding, gets a clear-out during building excavations between Aldermanbury and Godwin Street.

Rubbish piles up outside John Street Market during a dustmen's strike in the 1970s.

Members of Bradford CND march down Leeds Road in Thornbury in pouring rain in 1956, led by Bradford author John Braine (right) who wrote *Room at the Top*.

Somebody spilled the Tetley's: aftermath of a trolley bus accident on a summer evening in 1948 in Toller Lane. Happily nobody was hurt. In the background is the Coliseum cinema, which stood only yards from its rival, the Elite. In those days, in that part of town, there were at least four cinemas within a few minutes walk.

Bradford Muslims gather in the long, hot summer of 1976 to pray for rain. Britain was having one of its worst droughts on record. The prayer, during Ramadan, seems to have been answered – two days later it rained.

The Olympia Garage at the bottom of Thornton Road was always pretty busy. But it was more so in 1956 when the Suez Crisis curtailed fuel supplies. Motorists queued for 200 yards to buy petrol – two gallons maximum for 'regulars', one for others.

End of an era: Debenhams' store in Manningham Lane – formerly the much-liked Busbys – is destroyed by fire in 1979.

Debenhams' store fire: The clock, which had served a generation of Bradfordians, stands at high noon.

At Work

Chapter Two

Tub, 'posser', boiler, mangle and washboard – the equipment which meant it was washing day – usually Monday. And it was a long day.

Coin-operated launderettes and washing machines for the many were a long way in the future. There was the washhouse in Rupert Street, Little Horton, but here in 1969 the days of the municipally-owned laundry were numbered. Built at a cost of £57,000 in 1956, the washhouse was a godsend to housewives – but it wasn't profitable. It closed, despite tumultuous protests, including dirty washing being dumped on the steps of City Hall, in 1969. The coin-op launderettes had won.

These men helped give Bradford its most distinctive landmark – the 250 foot high Lister's Mill chimney. The picture was taken at the top shortly after completion in 1873. Lister toasted his future in Champagne at the top. Risky…

Left: The result: 8,000 tons of masonry towers above the skyline. Lister's Mill chimney can be seen from as far away as Ilkley Moor. It has been compared with the Campanile San Marco in Venice.

Right: Like father, like son: in the days of horse transport, the blacksmithing business often remained in the family for generations. Most villages and districts had more than one. Oddy's forge, seen here, kept horses in Tong village shod for many years. Wrought-iron gates and simpler things like hasps for padlocks were also their stock in trade.

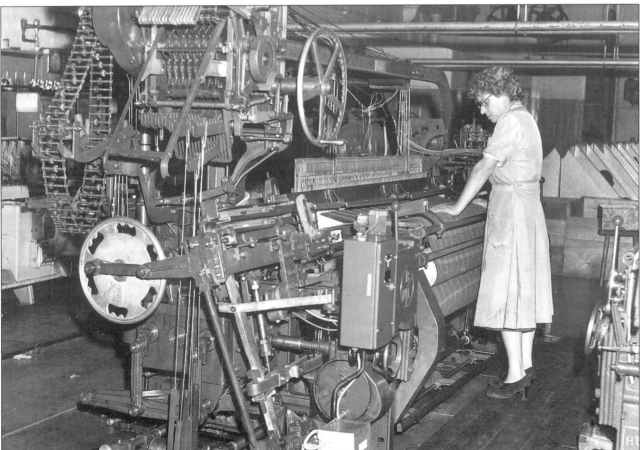

State of the art: The latest Northrop loom, which could weave four colours. It was installed at the mill of J.Speight & Sons & Co Ltd in 1960.

Fleeces from all over the world came to Bradford to be sorted. The idea was to produce 'matchings' which could be blended and made into worsted tops of various qualities. Whatever the quality, it was world renowned. The Ayatollah Khomeini was once photographed wearing a robe made at Hield Bros Ltd, of Brigella Mills, Bradford. A tyrant with taste…

Quality control: The first municipally-owned Conditioning House was opened in 1891 for 'ascertaining and certifying the true weight, length and condition of articles of the textile trade commonly used in the city'. The building here was opened in Canal Road in 1902. A certificate from the Conditioning House was as good as a banknote anywhere. If Bradford's testers said the quality was good, there was no arguing.

A breather: Workers from Bulmer and Lumb Ltd, Wibsey, worsted spinners and coloured top makers, take a break in the sun at lunchtime.

In a whirl: The latest ring spinning machine in action in 1964. More complex machinery meant fewer operators were needed.

Do-it-yourself: Manningham Mills employed a resident blacksmith in the early years of the century to carry out running repairs on machine parts.

The end: Workers at Thorn Consumer Electronics – formerly Bairds' – at Lidget Green leave the plant for the last time after its closure in 1978. 2,200 people in Bradford and Shipley lost their jobs.

On t'Change: In its heyday, Bradford's Wool Exchange had its pillars numbered so that woolmen could make appointments in an allotted place to meet and do business. Women were not allowed in.

Temple of Free Trade: The imposing vaulted ceiling of the Wool Exchange. Designed by Lockwood and Mawson – architects of the Town Hall – it was opened in 1897. The foundation stone was laid by the Prime Minister, Lord Palmerston, in 1864.

View from the top: Market Street, photographed from the tower of City Hall in 1973. At bottom left are Carters sports shop and the County Restaurant and Bars, now both gone. Top centre is the Wool Exchange.

Hazy spring: The banning of coal fires in the city in the early 1960s put paid to the smogs that were a plague and a danger. But even in 1968, this view across the city centre from Bolton Road shows evidence of industrial haze.

Exporting to the world: Horses and carts prepare to take Lister's products to the station for shipping. Barcelona and Buenos Aires were the destination of this consignment.

Lister's enters the motor age: A Lancashire & Yorkshire Railway truck picks up crates bound for Spain, Portugal and Egypt.

Big investment: The West Riding Worsted and Woollen Mills group invested £2m on new plant and equipment between 1961 and 1964. This state-of-the-art hank-to-cone winding machine was installed at Thomas Burnley & Sons Ltd, Bradford.

Update: The most modern weaving machine in the world at the time, installed at Scott (Dudley Hill) Ltd in the 1960s.

Organised chaos: Workers at Grattan, the huge Bradford mail-order company, dispatching goods in 1974.

Floral boost: Gardeners Brian Coulson and Charles Poulton White put the finishing touches to a clock honouring the Bradford Area Development Association in Bradford Moor Park in 1969.

The man who turned a 'white elephant' into a going concern: Osborne Sayer Wain, proprietor of 'Ossie' Wain's for more than 40 years. Nobody wanted the corner shop in Britannia House until Mr Wain turned it into Bradford's best known tailor's and outfitters, O.S.Wain. He died in 1962. His son, also O.S., carried on the business until it closed in 1987.

New body: The local government reforms of 1974, in which an enlarged Bradford became a metropolitan council, is marked by Lister Park's floral clock of that year.

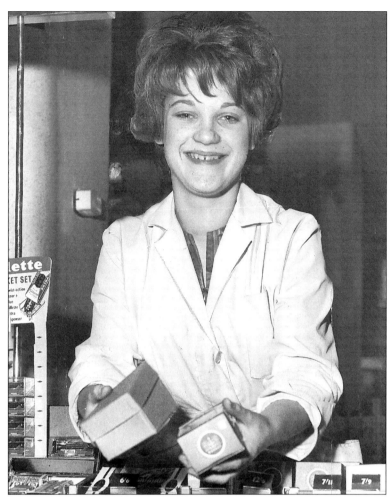

Great future: This shop assistant behind the counter at Boots in Broadway little knew what stardom lay ahead of her. She was an unknown Pauline Matthews until 1962 when, the day before this picture was taken, she stood in at an hour's notice for Donna Douglas in an Alhambra musical and wowed the audience. Later she changed her name to Kiki Dee.

Bradford has always been in the forefront of welfare work. The Bradford Hospital for the Sick Children of the Poor (later simply the Children's Hospital) in St Mary's Road, Manningham, opened in 1890. Samuel Cunliffe Lister, later Lord Masham, donated £5,000 of the £12,000 needed. The rest was raised by a vigorous committee of Bradford 'gentlewomen'. It closed in 1987.

Running round: Inside the circular ward – one of two – at Bradford Children's Hospital. The circular design made it easier for the duty nurse to keep an eye on all the patients.

One of the last saddlers in West Yorkshire was Fred Crowther, of Queensbury, who was in the business for nearly 60 years before his retirement in 1961 at the age of 79. He recalled that, when he was an apprentice, there were three blacksmiths making a living in the village.

In 1929, 91,709 animals were slaughtered in Bradford Abattoir. They found their way here to St James's Wholesale Meat Market, where the cobbles had to be scrubbed daily.

Noisy: The old Express Dairy in White Abbey Road in 1964. The sound of glass bottles being washed could be heard from quite a distance.

This was probably Bradford's best-known small shop – and rightly so. Philip Smith, the pork butchers in Ivegate, was renowned for its superb pies and sandwiches – and more. Here manager Peter Brambani (left) and David Ryan celebrate winning international trophies for their black puddings.

Big Demand: A typical pre-Christmas queue at Philip Smiths. A stand pie for Boxing Day was considered an essential part of the festive season.

At one time it was said that Bradford had more farmland inside its city boundaries than anywhere else in Britain. This farm is in Baldwin Lane, Clayton.

Heavy work: A stonemason poses at Vint's Quarry, Fagley, sometime in the late 1920s or early 1930s.

The Lord Lieutenant of the West Riding, the Earl of Scarborough (in uniform) had praise for the work-force of G.Garnet & Sons Ltd, at Apperley Bridge, in 1967. He was presenting the Queen's Award for Exports to the textile firm, saying its record was not only of benefit to the company, but to the country as well.

At School

Chapter Three

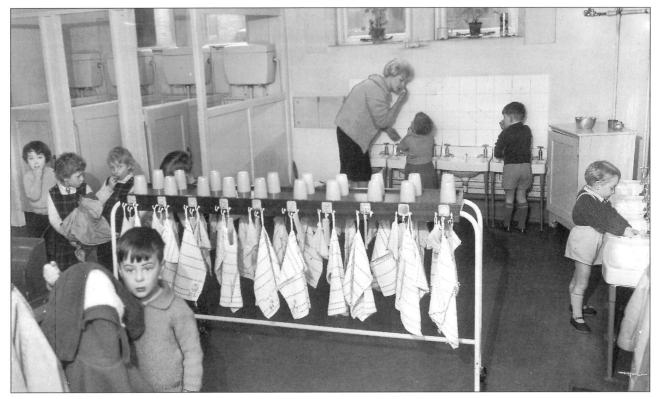

Lunchtime hand wash at Feversham Street Nursery School in 1963. The cloakroom of the 19th century building had just been refurbished.

Open for lessons: Bradford Education Chairman Alderman Tom Hall unveils a plaque marking the opening of the new Wellington Junior School at Eccleshill in 1969.

Here we go: Pupils of Allerton Modern School prepare for a day out to Pateley Bridge, Fountains Abbey and Brimham Rocks in 1946.

It was heads down – but with a few clandestine glances at the camera – at St Anthony's School, Clayton in 1954.

Belle Vue Boys' School in Manningham Lane, shortly after staff and pupils had moved up to Thorn Lane in Haworth Road in 1964. The girls – whose building was sandwiched between the junior and senior boys – moved to an adjoining site later.

The new Belle Vue Boys', opened in 1964, was set amid fields and woods. The bike sheds bottom left housed the tuck shop.

Proudly clutching certificates are pupils of Fox's School of Commerce, in Claremont, Bradford in the mid-1930s. The school was established in 1886 and lessons in economics, shorthand and typing fitted students for a life in the business world.

Queen for a day: Fairweather Green Infants' School celebrates May Day between the wars.

A breather: Mid-morning milk break for children at St Matthew's School, Allerton, in 1969.

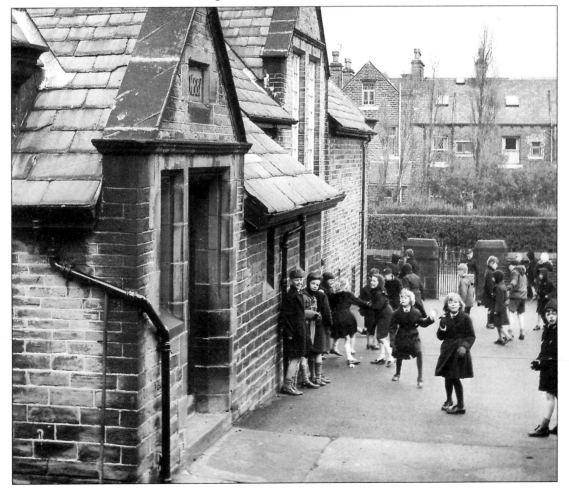

Playtime: Pupils of St Matthew's Church School, Bankfoot, enjoy the open air in the 1950s.

Playground hurley-burley at Windhill School in 1968.

Taped learning: The language laboratory at Lapage Middle School in the mid-1970s.

School's out: Home time at last for excited children at Lapage Middle.

Sporting arena: Horsfall Playing Fields, Woodside, scene of the annual inter-school athletics contest.

All the trimmings: A wartime Christmas for children at the Swain House Day Nursery.

Practical lesson: these three-year-olds at St Anne's Nursery School in Guy Street, Broomfield, Bradford in 1923 provided the senior girls at St Ann's with housewifery lessons. Every Friday the seniors came to the nursery to bathe the tots, wash their hair and weigh them. The nursery, meals included, cost parents half a crown (13p) a week.

Pioneering stuff: mixed gymnasium sessions were something of a novelty in the 1960s, but the new Fairfax School saw nothing wrong with the idea.

Thousands of Bradford schoolchildren took their first tentative steps into the water to learn to swim at Drummond Road Baths, seen here in 1968.

At Leisure

Chapter Four

Hot work: Children wait their turn to get at the drinking fountain which used to stand in Lister Park

Pioneer: Early Bradford motorist Stephen Johnson picnicking with friends on Clapham Common. The car is a 1906 Humber.

Snack time: Sandwiches, pie and peas and puddings offered a warm welcome to Baxandalls' café in the old
Kirkgate Market.

Photocall for Accent and players. The rock band were at Park Avenue to check the venue for a concert. The Bradford
Football Club players look disbelieving.

Fish fans: Thousands flocked to Harry Ramsden's at Guiseley when the famous restaurant celebrated its 21st birthday in 1952. Fish and chips were sold at the original prices for the day – three-halfpence (that's 0.625p).

Centre of attraction: A Granada TV camera crew filming in Bradford in 1956. They were in the area just before the opening of the ITA's second northern transmitter, at Emley Moor.

Tranquil: Chellow Dene Reservoir, near Allerton, caught in the aftermath of snow, is a popular walk within easy reach.

The Dagenham Girl Pipers perform at the opening of Fine Fare in Petergate in 1962. The supermarket had started life as Cooper's, the city's first.

His Majesty, a favourite of the crowds who watched trotting races at Greenfield Stadium, Dudley Hill in the early part of this century. Greenfield also hosted greyhound races.

The Cock and Bottle in Otley Road, Bradford, in 1906. If drinkers from that year walked into it today they would find it little changed. The woodwork, brass and stained glass remain intact.

It may have been a beautiful baby contest, or it may be a gathering of babies born at the same hospital. But they all watched the birdie here in the summer of 1932.

Monty the shire horse dressed and decorated by handler Harry Greenwood, celebrates May Day in 1957. Monty, owned by woolcombers J.F.Raspin Ltd, was taking part in a traditional procession.

Glory revealed: The Cartwright Hall, Lister Park, gleams in the autumn sunshine shortly after being cleaned in 1974.

A popular meeting place until it was demolished, Collinson's café boasted a string and piano trio in its heyday. The trio shrunk to a duo and later to a soloist – but the glorious smell of coffee wafting over the pavement never diminished.

Something for everyone: John Street open market in 1954. It seemed to sell everything from pigeons to plates, to pie and peas. And watching a crockery salesman seemingly carelessly flinging a dinner service in the air to display it was something of a treat for young shoppers.

The circus comes to town: Elephants lead the way for Billy Smart performers arriving for their annual visit to Peel Park in 1970.

Eyes on the skies: Huge crowds at the highly popular, annual air display at Yeadon Airport in 1959.

Sogged out: Heavy rain turned the alleys between Peel Park fairground attractions into a quagmire in the spring of 1969.

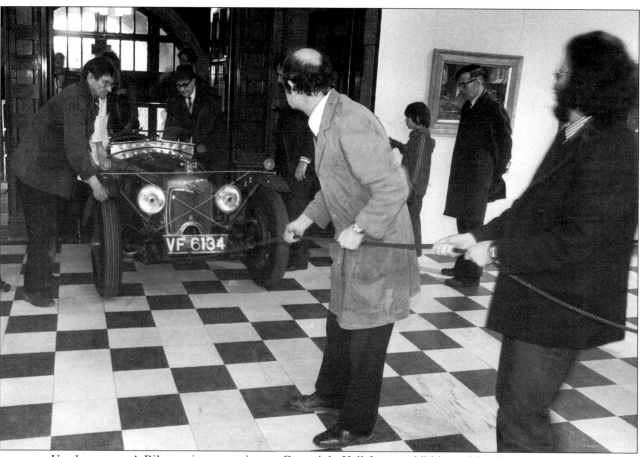

Up she comes: A Riley racing car arrives at Cartwright Hall for an exhibition celebrating motor sports.

During World War Two this building, at the junction of Little Horton Lane and Chester Street, was the headquarters of Bradford's Civil Defence. In the 1960s it became Glyde House, the headquarters of the Yorkshire Arts Association.

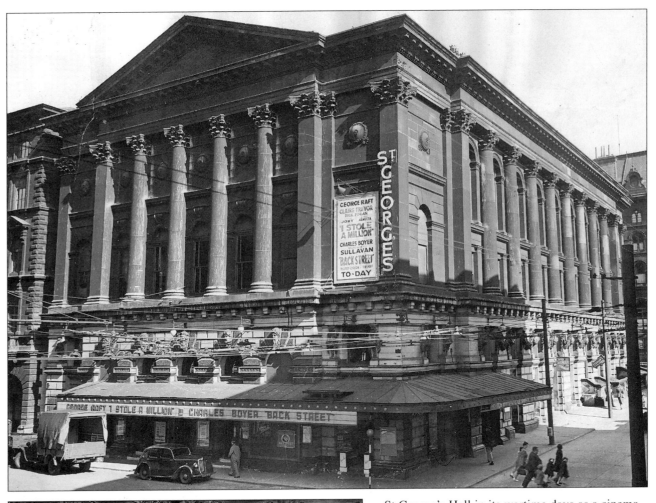

St George's Hall in its wartime days as a cinema.
Showing were George Raft in *I Stole a Million* and
Charles Boyer in *Back Street*.

Noted local naturalist Sidney
Jackson, keeper of the
Cartwright Hall, with a
collection of Celtic stone heads.
Some were found cemented
into pig sties and stables, others
were unearthed by gardeners.
The odd one even capped a
stone gatepost.

Instead of the galvanized metal bath on the floor of the front room – which most working people had to use – a shilling (5p) would buy a visit to baths like these at Tong Street, Dudley Hill in the 1950s.

A drinking fountain dedicated to the memory of Sir Robert Peel, champion and pioneer of the sort of free trade which enriched the city, in the park named after Peel in 1956.

Height of fashion: Members of the Pakistani Women's Association prepare for a fashion show at the then Bolton Royd College of Education – now part of Bradford and Ilkley Community College – in 1966. The dress rehearsal took place at the home of Mrs Masudah Ahmad (second from left).

Greeting: Bradford Hindus – and neighbours – celebrate the arrival of spring with a bonfire on the festival of Holi.

Light touch: Dancers celebrate Divali – the Hindu Festival of Light – in October 1976.

Whoa, there: A stage coach rattles along Broadway during the celebration in 1951 marking the 700th anniversary of the granting of market rights to Bradford.

Steady as she goes: An aqua-tandem is launched on the lake at Lister Park in the 1930s.

Hold tight: A young hero rescues a toy yacht on Lister Park's lake sometime in the 1920s.

Wheel's on fire: City Hall in the background as a ferris wheel picks up speed during the Blaise Fair at Bradford Arts Festival in 1971.

The Bradford Whit Walk attracted thousands of spectators to Peel Park to watch the road-walking race finish. These picnickers were photographed in the early 1920s.

Spring sunshine silhouettes carousel riders at the spring fair in Lister Park in 1979.

The Bradford Dolphins were a swimming club based at the Windsor Baths in Morley Street – but in 1978 the real thing was on show at the pool.

Stacked heels and flares date this immediately to the early 1970s. Midnight Lace entertain a crowd gathered on the cricket pitch at Park Avenue.

Food pioneer: The Lahore Restaurant in Lumb Lane in the 1960s. The Lahore, one of the first curry houses in the city, was where many native Bradfordians had their first taste of authentic Asian food – it has, happily, become a habit.

From Rolls-Royce to Austin A35, all parts of the social scale, providing they were car owners, pitched in to help with what was then – this is 1958 – rather brutally to modern ears called the Bradford Cripples' Outing. Drivers volunteered their services for the day and disabled people were taken to different destinations each year. The Bradford Cripples' Association became the Bradford and District Association for the Physically Disabled in 1962. But the outings continued.

Bradford-super-Mare: Morecambe sea front during the traditional Bradford Bowling Tide holiday week in 1954. It is more than likely that about one in five of the people in the picture hailed from the city. It was a favourite spot not only for holidays but for retirement – so much so that for many years the *T&A* maintained an office in the Lancashire resort to keep exiled Bradfordians in touch with their birthplace.

Tanning by numbers: In truth Morecambe was not exactly one of the world's great sun traps. But when it did come, you had to be quick to make sure of your place in it.

Showtime

Chapter Five

Showpiece: The ABC Ritz, opened in May 1939, was one of the most fashionable cinemas in the city centre. But as audiences fell it split its auditorium into twin screens, began to close on weekday afternoons, and finally closed in 1985.

Small but popular: The Oxford Cinema at Undercliffe was a much-loved local 'fleapit' before being turned into a bingo hall.

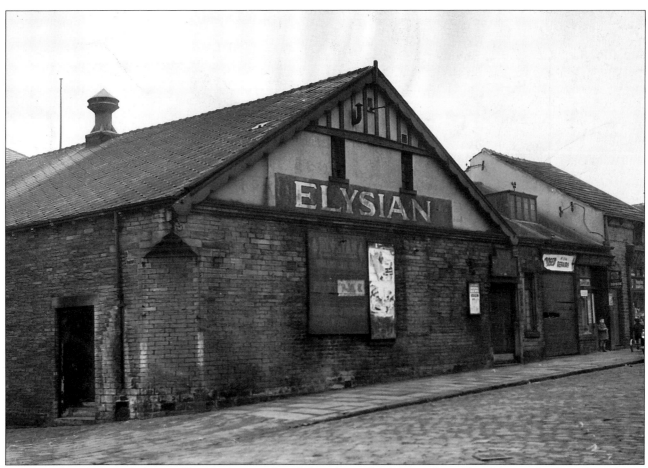

Lidget Green's 'other' cinema: The Elysian was dwarfed by the stylish brick and marble of the nearby Arcadian – but both attracted audiences.

Dual purpose: The Empire Cinema in Morley Street had opened as a theatre in 1899 but became a cinema in 1918. Later it was swallowed up by an extended Alexandra Hotel. And that, later, became an annexe of Bradford College.

Thronged: The Theatre Royal, between the wars, showing 'The biggest musical comedy success in London', *Mr Manhattan*. Along with the fine old Royal Standard pub next door to it, the theatre has disappeared.

Splendour: The circle foyer of the New Victoria, later the Gaumont and then the Odeon Twins. Built in 1930, it could seat 3,300 people and as well as a cinema was also a popular live concert venue.

Lost Empire: The crumbling interior of the Bradford Empire just before its demolition in 1957.

Panto time: The Alhambra Theatre in 1952 at Christmas. Pantomime always drew the crowds and a great favourite, Jack Storey, starred in this production. The theatre, built by Francis Laidler, was begun in 1912. It officially opened on Wednesday, 18 March 1914, a gleaming cream-coloured building. Bradford variety audiences were notoriously tough on comedians and one day George Formby Senior (father of the gap-toothed, ukulele-playing comic) nodded towards the gleaming domes and said "Anyway, yon's a fine tombstone for a comic".

The shock of the new: The refurbished Alhambra Theatre reflected in the city's Central Police Headquarters.

Young stars: The Sunbeams, a locally recruited chorus line, always enchanted audiences. This troupe is in the 1952
Mother Goose.

The Bishop of Bradford, Dr Alfred W.F.Blunt, visiting the Alhambra dressing room of Norman Evans, one of the greatest
pantomime dames of all time.

Left: The Redgraves are probably the largest acting dynasty Britain has ever produced. Their well-known member, Vanessa, is seen here braving the rain while filming *Yanks* in the district in 1978.

Right: Another great dame: Bunny Doyle, panto star and comedian, pictured dressed in the *Yorkshire Observer* in the 1955 Alhambra panto.

Boys in the band: The Bradford Theatre Royal and Opera House orchestra pictured in 1896.

We want the Stones:
Teenagers prepare to camp out
on the steps of the Gaumont to
be first in the queue for tickets
for a Rolling Stones concert in
1965.

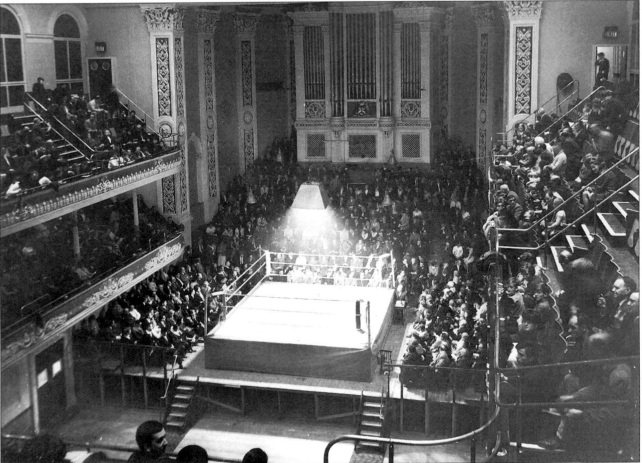

St George's Hall ready for a wrestling match in 1966. Showjumper Harvey Smith was among the competitors.

'Mr Halle's Band' was always a welcome visitor to Bradford. Here, in a 1972 subscription concert, the Halle Orchestra is conducted by James Loughran.

Musical day out: Members of the Bradford Vocal Union on the promenade at Morecambe before performing at the Winter Gardens Musical Festival Jubilee in 1954.

Pen pal on points: Royal Ballet soloists Deirdre O'Conair (left) and Doreen Wells explain some of the art of dance to pupils from Undercliffe Secondary School, backstage at the Alhambra Theatre in 1964. The children had been penfriends with Miss O'Conair through their teacher, Miss E.M.Ibbotson, after she had stayed with her during an earlier visit.

Legendary line-up. Rock stars Gene Vincent and Eddie Cochran lined up at the Gaumont in 1960. The dearest tickets were 7/6d (38p). Cochran would not return after this January visit. He died in a car crash in April of the same year.

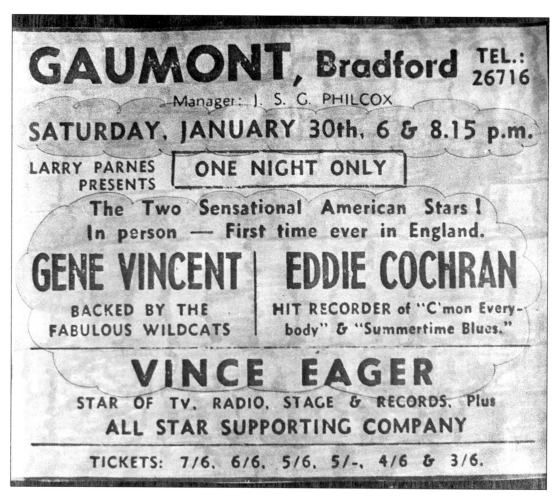

GAUMONT, Bradford TEL.: 26716

Manager: J. S. G. PHILCOX

SATURDAY, JANUARY 30th, 6 & 8.15 p.m.

LARRY PARNES PRESENTS — ONE NIGHT ONLY

The Two Sensational American Stars !
In person — First time ever in England.

GENE VINCENT | **EDDIE COCHRAN**

BACKED BY THE FABULOUS WILDCATS | HIT RECORDER of "C'mon Everybody" & "Summertime Blues."

VINCE EAGER

STAR OF TV, RADIO, STAGE & RECORDS, Plus

ALL STAR SUPPORTING COMPANY

TICKETS: 7/6, 6/6, 5/6, 5/-, 4/6 & 3/6.

John Braine, Bradford-born author of *Room at the Top*, places a sealed lead casket in the wall of Bingley Little Theatre's new premises, formerly the town's ambulance headquarters, in 1973.

Sporting Life
Chapter Six

Conquering heroes: Bradford City's FA Cup-winning side of 1911. After a 0-0 draw at the Crystal Palace, City won the replay against Newcastle United at Maine Road, Manchester, with a single goal from skipper Jimmy Spiers (third from left, middle row). It would be nice to say it was a triumph for Yorkshire grit, but in truth there wasn't an Englishman in the side. They were either Scots or Irish.

Night moves: Bradford Northern train under floodlights in 1951. The lights, mounted on the rim of both stands at Odsal, were something of a novelty.

Starting over: The Odsal pitch is ripped up in 1968 to improve the drainage. Before the advent of the four- – then six- – tackle law, watching Rugby League could be a dour experience as forwards 'shoved the ball up their jumpers' and battled yard by yard down the middle in a quagmire.

Above and overleaf, top: It started out as the Odsal Sports Centre – then Richard Dunn earned himself a crack at the world heavyweight title against Muhammad Ali in Germany while work was still in progress. He gave a determined if unsuccessful account of himself, and certainly didn't let his native city down. So the centre, seen here taking shape, now bears his name.

Faded pride: Grass grows uncontrolled on the pitch at Park Avenue in 1973. The Bradford Football Club were ejected from the Football League in 1970 after too many seasons propping up the Fourth Division. But the loyalty of their fans was remarkable, and local derbies with Bradford City had a special atmosphere.

Traditional weather for a Yorkshire match at Park Avenue in the 1970s. Purists reckoned if it didn't rain, some of the atmosphere on Sir Len Hutton's favourite ground was missing. The football stand at the back was regarded by many as the finest spot on any county cricket ground to watch the game. You were behind and above the bowler's arm and missed nothing. And you stayed dry…

Paperwork: One of the most wholehearted players ever to put on a Yorkshire sweater finds GCE exams less appealing than keeping wicket. Bradford-born David Bairstow got special permission to take his exams early in the morning in 1970 because he was playing at Park Avenue for the county. He went on to take five catches in a drawn match, then went on to play for England and captain his county. His son Andrew went on to play for Derbyshire. He also played League football with Bradford City in the 1970s.

Fast curve: A demonstration of speed skating at the newly-opened Silver Blades Ice Rink in Bradford in 1966.

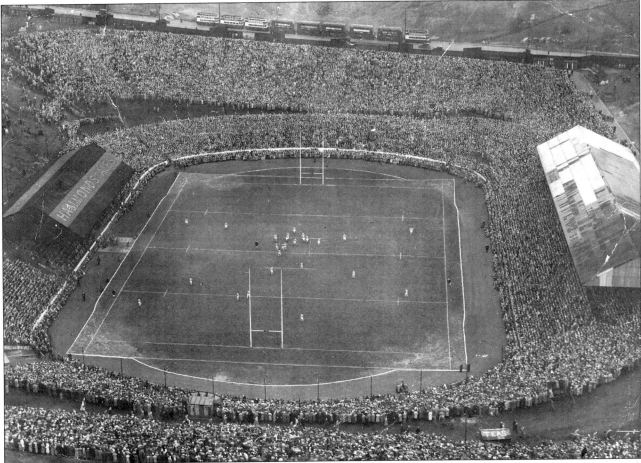

The world record crowd for a Rugby League match at Odsal in 1954 – and Northern weren't even playing! The replay of
the Challenge Cup Final between Halifax and Warrington attracted 102,569 fans. Warrington won 8-4.

Respects: Members of Leeds and Bradford Ex-Professional Boxers' Association gather in Bowling cemetery at the renovated grave of Jerry Delaney, a Bradford boxer killed in World War One. Father Anthony Hinnighan rededicated the grave in 1960.

The Roses Match, especially when Yorkshire were in their pomp, was a highly-attractive fixture. Here, police have to force the Park Avenue gates shut on would-be spectators in the 1930s after the ground was full.

One world champion and one future world champion clashed at the Bradford Snooker Centre in 1975. Alex Higgins (right) was in town to play Bradford's own Joe Johnson. Higgins had won the world title in 1972 – Joe was to win it in 1986.

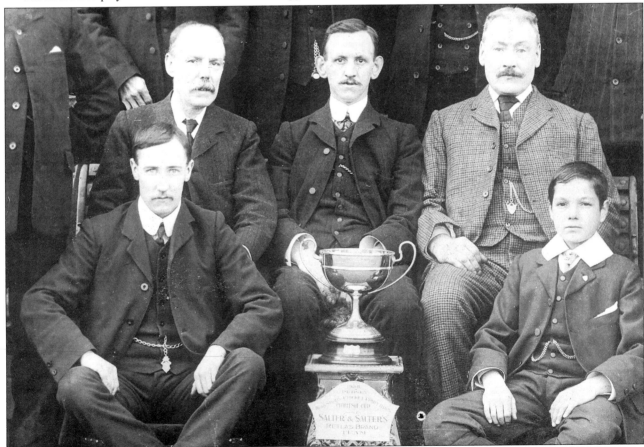

The lad on the front right could not have dreamed what the future held for him: a record first-wicket partnership of 555 for Yorkshire and adulation as one of England's finest opening batsmen. The young Herbert Sutcliffe is seen here as a member of a Pudsey workshop team.

Bradford Northern captain Ernest Ward introduces the team to King George VI before the 1948 RL Challenge Cup Final at Wembley. Northern got to the Final three years on the trot, in 1947, 1948 and 1949, winning twice. Not this game, though. They lost 8-3 to Wigan. Like everybody else, later…

Sir Leonard Hutton's favourite ground – Park Avenue in Bradford. The great batsman liked the intimacy of the ground – and the fact it had short boundaries.

Top tips: Dennis Viollet, of Manchester United, one of the survivors of the Munich disaster, visits Sooty's Shop in Bradford in 1960 to demonstrate a new table top football game.

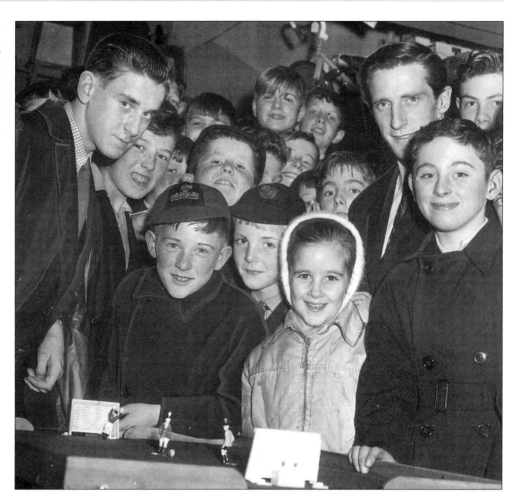

Early heroes: Boxing gear was rather elementary back in 1913. The man on the right was called Bramley, and the man standing behind him was his brother Tom, a very fine bowls player in his time.

Face-out: Bradford boxer Richard Dunn refuses to be intimidated by Muhammad Ali at the weigh-in for their world heavyweight title fight in Munich in 1976. Dunn lost, but gave a good account of himself.

Well tried: City Hall puts out a banner for Richard Dunn after Munich. He was welcomed back by a civic reception, and hundreds of cheering fans.

Winners again: The Yorkshire side which took the County Championship title in 1963. Back row (left to right): Doug Padgett, John Hampshire, Don Wilson, Mel Ryan, Tony Nicholson, Bryan Stott, Phil Sharpe. Front row: Jimmy Binks, Fred Trueman, Brian Close (captain), Ray Illingworth and Ken Taylor.

…And again: The 1967 champions. Back row (left to right): Geoff Cope, Phil Sharpe, Tony Nicholson, Peter Stringer, John Waring, John Hampshire and Geoff Boycott. Front row: Doug Padgett, Jimmy Binks, Fred Trueman, Brian Close (captain), Ray Illingworth, Ken Taylor and Don Wilson. The side contained three men who would captain England.

All Change

Chapter Seven

One of Bradford's best-loved buildings, the elegant Swan Arcade in Market Street, before its demolition in 1962.

Shattered: Workmen with crowbars begin the demolition of the arcade in March 1962. The destruction aroused much anger, particularly from Bradford-born author J.B.Priestley, who had worked there as a youth.

The wrought iron and marbled interior of Swan Arcade. This is part of the North Avenue.

Councillors and officials tour Southfield Square, off Lumb Lane, in 1976. The square, with its central gardens and Victorian terraces, was threatened with demolition, but a vigorous local campaign was mounted to save it. Protesters pointed out that the square had historic value, was truly multi-racial, multi-cultural and – above all – friendly. Money was found, work was done and the square survives to this day (below) at the heart of a community which is on the up.

The double frontage of Busbys – 'The store with the friendly welcome' – in its heyday in the 1950s.

The extensions to Bradford Cathedral stand out starkly against the older parts as work went on in 1961.

Old shops and other property in Westgate in 1951. All was to come down in the great redevelopment in the 1960s.

Trolley bus wires and bus stop are a reminder of a quiet, fast mode of transport. This is Clayton Road, Lidget Green in 1958.

The new Central Library Theatre takes shape during a major reshaping of the city in the 1960s. It later became the luxury cinema Pictureville.

Sign of change: 1974 and the new local government set-up enlarged Bradford, bringing in towns like Bingley, Shipley and Keighley, which had up to then had their own councils.

Ready for the hammer: Houses in Binbrook Street, Four Lane Ends, stand waiting for slum clearance.

Green field site: A view of Bradford from Prospect Mills, painted by Charles Cundall, gives an idea of what the city was like in the last century.

When wool was king: A view across central Bradford before the days of smoke control. The resulting smogs could be deadly.

Bird's eye view of a changing cityscape in 1968. City Hall is at top left and the Odeon, bottom left, with the Alhambra on its right-hand side. The Central Library and Wardley House dominate the right-hand side with Chester Street Bus Station at bottom right.

Working on the night-shift under floodlights are the men building the new Bradford Institute of Technology in 1960. Six years later it became the University.

What might have been: An early 1960s projected plan for the rebuilding of Bradford's city centre. Even this modernistic looking idea did not envisage the rail linking of the two stations.

The only old building which remains from the time this picture was taken in Hall Ings is the Jacob's Well pub. Later it would be joined by the Interchange and Metrochange House.

Standard, Austin, Morris and Sunbeam – all cars from a different era. It was 1957 and Rawson Place was echoing to the sound of building work on the meat and vegetable market.

Lost cinema: The Cosy in Wibsey High Street, closed in the 1960s. It was flanked by two outfitters, the one on the right being a well-known Bradford name – O.S.Wain. 'Ossie' Wain had his main store at the corner of Bridge Street and Market Street in the city centre.

Changing skyline: A night photograph taken in 1960 from the top of the *T&A* building shows the then Ritz cinema and the work going ahead on what would become the Wolfe and Hollander building on the right.

Vanishing shops: Darley Street in 1968 with household names like Jackson the Tailor, Craven Dairies, John Collier and – biggest loss of all – F.W. Woolworth.

Bradford is surrounded by stone quarries from which local houses and businesses were built. But Dudley Hill boasted this brickworks up until the 1950s.

Exchange Station, built in the 1880s for the Lancashire & Yorkshire Railway, seen here decked out in honour of the Coronation of the Queen in 1953.

The trains had gone from the old Exchange Station after the Travel Interchange was built on the other side of Bridge Street. The space relieved the pressure on a city chronically short of parking space.

Soot from 90 years of steam locomotion flies as the demolition men start to pull Exchange Station down in 1976.

Slipper baths, Turkish baths, sunray treatment, saunas – oh, and swimming – were all available at the Windsor Baths, now closed, in Morley Street.

High Emotion: Mohammed Ajeeb with his father at Ajeeb's inauguration as Bradford – and Britain's – first Lord Mayor of Asian origin. Representatives of many racial backgrounds – including Irish, Jewish, Scottish and Welsh – have made their contributions to our civic life.

North Parade in happier times, in 1969, when trade was brisk and traffic was able to travel in both directions, and to park. Traders today have it harder.

The cobbles ringing to the sound of horseshoes was a familiar one at the time of the Coronation of Edward VII in 1902.
Here Kirkgate Market is dressed for the occasion.

Nearly over: Kirkgate Market bustles with activity in 1972 – but its fate was sealed and demolition loomed on the horizon.

The end: Kirkgate's market stalls are shrouded for the last time in November 1973. Demolition began the day after its closure.

A soot-shrouded Wool Exchange is in stark contrast to the newly-cleaned City Hall in 1968. When the Exchange was finally cleaned, a handsome sandstone and pink granite building emerged.

Lost brews:
Manchester Road,
one of Bradford's
most-pubbed
thoroughfares,
with signs of
three local beers
which have
vanished –
Hammonds,
Ramsdens and
Heys.

Steamy: The view from Wapping across Bolton Road and the vanished Canal Road cooling towers. Lister's Mill
dominates the distant skyline.

Gaslamps and cobbles in Ivegate in the 1920s. On the right is the Unicorn Inn, which closed its doors in the 1980s. In the distance is the Grosvenor Hotel, later a Berni Inn, and now the Ram's Revenge.

Living over the shop was once way of life for most tradesmen. And the local shop was a community institution. Here in Legrams Lane, at the junction with Cumberland Road, you could drop into a chemist's, a greengrocers, a clothing shop and a shoe repairers – all within 100 yards.

Back o' t'mill: Valley Street, originally built to house workers at Raspin, the commission woolcombers which dominates the end of the street, was demolished in 1961.

The Old Number One Court at Bradford City Hall. Both magistrates and Recorders (judges at Quarter Sessions) sat on the bench.

New face: Sunwin House, the headquarters of the Bradford and District Co-operative Society, at the junction of Sunbridge Road and Godwin Street, the day before its opening in 1963.

As the sun sinks slowly in the west... whatever benefits the Clean Air Act brought to the city, it meant the end of spectacular sunsets like this one in 1960.

Out of the rubble: from Ripley Street, West Bowling, over the railway sidings, the new high-rise flats at the bottom of Manchester Road in 1968.

Big enterprise: The foundation stone for Bradford's new Town Hall, designed by Lockwood and Mawson, who were also architects of the Wool Exchange, is laid in 1870.

Great works: A new skyline emerges in the centre of Bradford in the late 1960s. The Central Library and Wardley House had opened recently, and the inner ring road was open to traffic. On the left, the foundations of the city's new magistrates' court are being laid.

Surrounded by shanty shops, Paper Hall, one of Bradford's oldest buildings, was in a sorry state here in 1972 . Fortunately there were enthusiasts on hand to clamour for its preservation. The recent picture (below) shows the transformation.

The superb St John's Methodist Church in Wilmer Road, Heaton. The scaffolding around the spire was to support the tip, which high winds had blown over at an angle. The church is now used by Ukrainian worshippers.

Non-conformist churches outnumbered all other denominations many times over in Bradford. Horton Bank Methodist Church opened a new Sunday school, seen here, in 1962.

The German immigrants who helped to bring wealth to the city in the 19th century also brought their own brand of faith, represented here in the German Evangelical Church in Great Horton Road.

Place of worship: Sikhs in the Guru Nanak Temple in Wakefield Road. They bought the former Methodist hall in 1970 for over £9,000 and converted it.

Overflow into Leeds Road as Eastbrook Hall, the Methodist mission, opened in 1903. It stood on the site of the earlier
Eastbrook Chapel.

Patriarchal: The heavily bearded figure of Sir Titus Salt surveys the goings-on outside the then Town Hall in the last century. As the city centre changed, the statue was moved to Lister Park, where it still stands.

Wash and brush up for Sir Robert Peel in 1957. The statue of the founder of the modern police force used to stand in Peel Square. Right: Peel Square in 1951, with Peel's statue dominant.

W E.Forster brought low. The statue of the founder of universal education was removed from his old spot in the square named after him in 1963 and moved to another part of the redeveloping square.

At War
Chapter Eight

Members of the Auxiliary Fire Service (sometimes referred to as Auntie Fanny's Sunbeams) parade past City Hall during World War Two.

Ready for anything: The men of the Salt's (Saltaire) fire brigade prepare to go into action in 1939.

Troops and tanks line up outside City Hall during a military flag-waver and fund-raiser in 1941.

Post C of the Bradford Air Raid Precautions unit, with gleaming helmets, pose during World War Two.

Waiting for Hitler: Members of the Crossflatts Home Guard company, pictured in front of the sports pavilion at Bingley Grammar School.

Pilots of 609 (West Riding) Squadron of the RAF, pose with a piece of metal salvaged from a German Ju88 bomber shot down in 1940.

Wartime Prime Minister Winston Churchill prepares to address Bradford from the steps of City Hall in 1942. With him are his wife Clementine and daughter Lt Mary Churchill.

The people of Tyersal wave flags to show they can take it despite their damaged homes after an air raid in 1940.

Bystanders survey the damage caused by a bombing raid in Brunswick Street, Manchester Road in 1941.

Monument at Scholemoor Cemetery commemorating the six firemen who died in the massive explosion at Low Moor munition works in 1916 during World War One.

Wartime scrap brass salvaged from Bradford households is stacked up at the Cleansing Depot in Hammerton Street. It would go to make munitions.

Ready to do their bit: Number 2 Platoon of A Company, the Bradford Pals Battalion assemble in a Bradford Park in 1914. In 1916 the First Battle of the Somme would see terrible carnage among young men who, in many cases, lived in the same street, had been at school and worked together.

Casualties of War: Double page of pictures of local men killed or wounded during the Battle of the Somme in July 1916. Similar displays were in the *Bradford Daily Telegraph* from July until Christmas.

Survivors: A 1984 reunion of World War One veterans gather at the RAF Association Club in Mill Lane, Bradford.

While Bradford got off comparatively lightly from the attentions of Hitler's bombers, there were attacks on the city. Lingard's store and the Odeon Cinema in Manchester Road were among the buildings damaged. However, housewives here give an unmistakable message of solidarity to the Nazis.

Laid up: The Provost of Bradford, the Very Revd Alan Cooper, with the colours of the 6th Battalion the West Yorkshire Regiment, which were laid up in Bradford Cathedral in 1963. The battle honours listed begin in 1695 with the fighting at Namur in the War of the Grand Alliance. The most significant name is that of the Somme in 1916. On the first day of that battle, the Bradford Pals took part. They were among 60,000 British troops who lay dead, dying or wounded by midday.

When will they ever learn? Two small lads ponder the meaning of Bradford's war memorial. The year was 1939, and the boxes the boys are carrying show the sadness inherent in the picture. They are gas mask cases and, not 20 years after World War One, World War Two had begun.

Members of Bradford's Sikh Community, who fought in World War Two, remember VE Day on its 40th anniversary in 1985.

Lest we forget: Remembrance Day ceremony at the Bradford Cenotaph in 1962. The picture was taken from the roof of the Alhambra Theatre.

In Uniform

Chapter Nine

The Bradford Police scooter patrol rehearse for their Whitsuntide exhibition in Lister Park in 1960.

Drums and bugles: Inaugurating the 26th Company (Bradford Cathedral) Boys Brigade in about 1940.

As the volume of traffic negotiating the city centre increased, police on point duty were fitted with white coats and a white helmet cover to make them more visible in 1961.

Bradford has always regarded itself as a rather loose agglomeration of villages which somehow evolved into a city. But one village name always amuses outsiders. Here, at the turn of the century, are the men of the Idle Fire Brigade.

The vision of Sir Titus Salt, founder of Saltaire, embraced not only work but welfare, education, sport and culture. This is the Salts Silver Band pictured in the village in 1931.

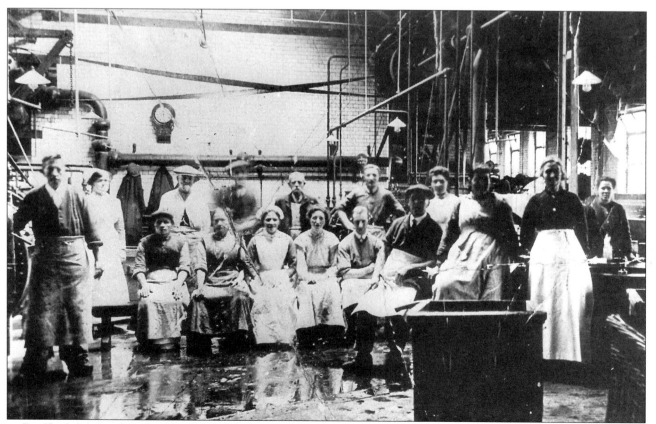

Bradford rightly prides itself on its social pioneering with an enviable list of firsts in things like school meals, school dentistry, school clinics. Its health care has always been in the forefront, too, but with a stream of war-wounded from the trenches in January 1918, these workers in the washhouse at St Luke's Hospital must have been feeling not a little shell-shocked themselves.

Smart turnout: The Lord Lieutenant of the West Yorkshire, Sir William Bulmer, inspects the band at the opening of the new Belle Vue Barracks in 1983.

The City of Bradford police force had a proud record as an independent organisation from its inception, However, as they paraded through the city here in 1971, the end was in sight. In 1974, after local government reform, they became bound up with the West Yorkshire force.

A band of guardsmen march along Market Street sometime in the early 1950s. It is possibly at the time when an army unit was being granted the Freedom of the City – which conferred the right to parade with fixed bayonets.

It's a woman's life… An Army careers convention at Bradford University in 1971 attracted a lot of female interest.

Led by pipes and drums, volunteer soldiers of the 272 Field Support Squadron of the Royal Engineers parade during the ceremony giving them the Freedom of the City in 1979.

Above: Pay parade at Thornbury Barracks for Territorials of the 4th Battalion, the Parachute Regiment in 1967. TA volunteers were paid an annual bounty of up to £100 – a tidy sum then. The poppy behind Corporal M.Fisher's cap badge indicates the time of year – it was just after Remembrance Day.

Left: End of the Swinging Sixties: Bradford Army Cadets from Belle Vue Barracks train on the formidable assault course at Strensall Barracks, near York in 1970.

Mark of respect: Lord Mayor Alderman Tom Hall unveils a plaque in Bradford Cathedral commemorating the service of the Bradford Borough Police and the City of Bradford Police, who became part of the new West Yorkshire force on local government reform in 1974.

On the Move
Chapter Ten

One of Bradford's best-known landmarks, the Exchange Station, with its two arched roofs, just before demolition began in 1976. The new Interchange terminal (foreground) had replaced it.

The new Yorkshire Pullman prepares to leave Exchange Station in 1961. It linked Bradford with London King's Cross, and British Railways were so pleased that they put the first and second class coaches on show to the public.

Resplendent in bowler hat and formal topcoat, stationmaster Mr Wilfred Ellaby sees his last train out of Exchange Station in 1970. He was retiring after 49 years on the railways.

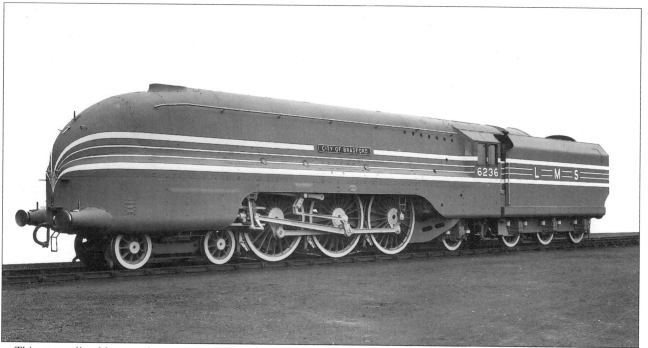

This streamlined locomotive, named after the city – one of several over the years – went into service with the London Midland Scottish line in 1939, only a few weeks before war broke out. Its colourful livery would soon be covered in black paint.

Another *City of Bradford*, this one in 1948 being owned by the newly-nationalised British Railways.

When wool ruled the city's economy, the railways were a vital link between seaports and the interior. Once raw materials arrived at the station, teams of horses were needed to get them to the mills. The stables here were the Midland Company's at Frizinghall.

Road transport took many forms in the 1920s when Bradford Corporation introduced this trackless electric truck.

Historic moment at the turn of the century, when the first electric tram arrived in Thornton.

Changing colours: dark blue and a later light blue tram pass the Mechanics Institute in 1947. At the time the institute was showing films.

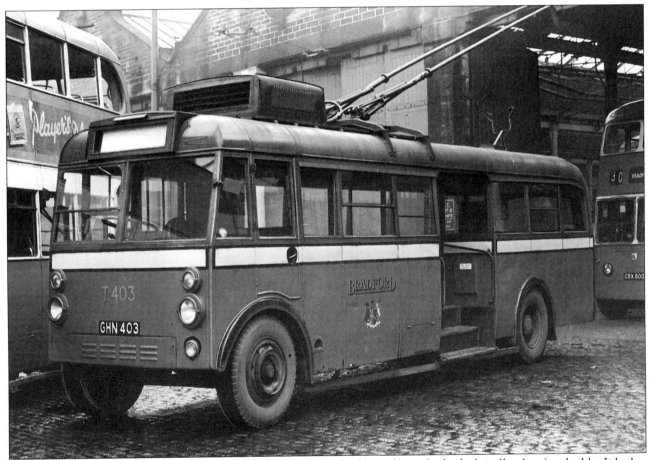

The fuel shortage which followed the Suez Crisis in 1956 made this curious, single-deck trolley-bus invaluable. It had been bought from Darlington Corporation to be broken up for spare parts, but it ended up as part of the double-deck fleet.

Bradford – and Britain's – last trolley-bus leaves the city centre for a ceremonial journey to Thornton in 1972. Hundreds of enthusiasts lined the route.

Up for sale: The former Duckworth Lane Bus Depot, which closed in the 1970s and was put on the market in 1977.

Busy route: Overshadowed by Wardley House, Chester Street Bus Station, depot for West Yorkshire's Bradford-based fleet, is pictured in 1973. A small café in the corner, beneath the bus crews' rest room, was a warm refuge on wintry days.

August Bank Holiday Monday at Exchange Station, with trains bound for coast or country. But the bread still had to be delivered. Bottom right is one of the endearing Scammel 'Iron Horse' towing trucks.

Bradford's Forster Square Station concourse in 1962. The terminal also housed a busy parcels depot.

Bradford's other station: The Adolphus Street terminal built for the Leeds, Bradford & Halifax Junction Railway in 1855. It was taken over by the Great Northern Railway but was too far out of the city centre and closed to passengers in 1867. It still handled goods in this picture from 1957.

Why Forster Square got its name:
The stature of W.E.Forster MP,
pioneer of universal education,
points to the station which now
bears his name in the 1890s. In
front of him is the statue of
William Oastler, defender of child
factory workers. It now stands in
Northgate.

Before buses, trams and trolleys: A replica stage coach arrives to meet Bradford's first train in a re-enactment at the 1947
Centenary Pageant in Peel Park.

Railway bosses admire the new turntable installed at Forster Square Station in 1938.

Journey's end – or beginning. The café and lounge at Forster Square Station in 1966. It was popular, and not only with rail travellers. A decent breakfast could be had there.

Vanishing City

Chapter Eleven

Hemmed in: Until the 1960s, most citizens of Bradford had only a vague idea of what their City Hall looked like overall. Snowden's Corner, seen here in 1962, was one of the buildings that stretched up almost to its walls.

There are no flat roads out of Bradford. Otley Road, seen here from Tennyson Place in the 1930s, winds up until it passes between Undercliffe Cemetery and Peel Park. On the left is a pawnbroker's shop, and on the right a local branch of Boots the chemists.

Noted for its brass, woodwork, stained glass and mosaic floors – and live music and a pretty good pint, too – the Royal Standard in Manningham Lane, near the Theatre Royal, seen here in 1977 closed and was demolished after a fire in 1991.

The end for Wallers old brewery near Trafalgar Street in the centre of Bradford. It had ceased brewing in 1916, but lasted in various guises until 1953.

T' Mucky Beck – Bradford's own rivulet – exposed during building work in 1959 opposite the Swan Arcade in Market Street. A tendency to flood and to smell (hence the nickname) made the beck more of a curse than a blessing in the early part of the century.

Dangerous job: Two demolition workers were hurt while clearing old housing in Barkerend Road in 1978. In the background is what was then Hanson School.

New face: Hall Ings gets ready for massive changes in 1964. The dotted line shows where the Norfolk Gardens Hotel was to be built. The premises of T.C.Firth Ltd and John L.Morley were to go, as was the old Queen Hotel in Bridge Street (left).

Outside middens, gas lamps and dumped rubbish: Ripon Street, off Otley Road, prepares to disappear in 1966.

Only the building on the left gives a clue to where this was. It is the bottom of Leeds Road in the 1950s, and the Ritz Cinema is in its heyday. The 72 Leeds-Bradford bus waits at a pedestrian crossing.

The pneumatic drills arrive and Broadway begins to become a pedestrians-only precinct in 1971.

Snowden's Corner has gone in 1963, City Hall's south face stands revealed and the way is clear for Norfolk Gardens, a breath of open space in a hitherto huddled city centre.

The New Inn, a coaching station in its early days, in Tyrrel Street, in the early 1960s. Auctions, inquests and even the occasional magistrates' hearing were held there in its heyday, and it was a popular and busy pub to the end.

Vital link: In the 18th century, before the advent of the railways, canals were the most efficient way to move heavy goods. Bradford was connected by a spur to the Leeds & Liverpool Canal at Shipley. Spinkwell Lock and its gates, near Wapping, were still more or less intact here in the early 1950s, but the notoriously smelly canal had been drained when the faster railway system replaced it.

An economy founded on mills meant chimneys. But the city diversified and other businesses began to make their contribution, many chimneys had to go. This one at Listerhills was blown down for work on extensions at the Grattan mail order empire.

Appropriate name: The Cuba Café, on the sixth floor of the Lloyds Bank Chambers in Hustlergate, had a neat promotional gimmick. If you went in and bought a cigar you got the accompanying coffee free. It was popular rendezvous after Exchange business for woolmen for 150 years until it closed in 1969. Its passing was mourned, but there must be souvenirs still around. The well-worn chairs, many over 100 years old, were offered for sale to customers as mementoes.

Under t'clock: The charge desk and reception room to the cells at the old Bradford police headquarters at City Hall in 1969. The wooden bench and bars must have made a few hearts sink.

For most of human history, the speed of a galloping horse was the maximum speed for communication. Then came the railways. For the first time for many people it was possible actually to see the world outside their own neighbourhood. Bradford's rail network was extensive and – considering the hills – impressive. Dudley Hill Station is seen here in the early 1950s, when there was still a single line handling freight.

Apart from the two-tone, single-deck bus, little has changed here since the 1930s. The main gate to Lister Park at the bottom of Oak Lane, and Lister's statue, remain. The bus, although petrol-driven, was still run under the authority of Bradford City Tramways.

Road in waiting: Wakefield Road, Dudley Hill in 1968, after whole rows of houses had been demolished to make way for the road-widening scheme which would link Bradford to the nation's motorway network.

In the way: the redevelopment of Wakefield Road in the late 1960s meant several landmarks had to go. Here, auctioneer Mr J.R.Hepper, in bowler hat, takes bids for equipment at a snowy Greenfield Stadium, beloved of greyhound racing enthusiasts, in 1969. Below: The stadium in its heyday.

By 1959, dealers at the annual Wibsey Horse Fair had been predicting the end of the traditional event. Not enough horses were changing hands, although there was no shortage of spectators here in Folly Hall Road.

The chimney at Oakroyd Dyeworks in Thornton Road, Bradford, is felled after a fire in 1984.

The Theatre Tavern, in
Manningham Lane, took its
name from the fact it was
next to the Theatre Royal.
The pub came down for the
road widening scheme which
linked Westgate,
Manningham Lane and
Canal Road, via Hamm
Strasse.

Demolition in the Leeds Road area in 1969. The council had decided that back-to-back houses with outside middens and multi-storey tenements were no longer wanted.

Thornville, the preparatory school for Bradford Grammar in Keighley Road, sees its final days in 1974. The land had been bought by Bradford and Northern Housing to build flats. All was not lost – ornate plasterwork from the Victorian mansion was rescued and went to Bolling Hall.

Major road works ahead: Bridge Street is blocked in 1964 during the reshaping of Bradford's city centre. The main casualty was the Mechanics' Institute, behind the bus in the background.

Circling the square: Bustle around the shops of Victoria Square in 1950. The New Victoria cinema was showing *The Eagle and the Hawk*, with John Payne and Rhonda Fleming.

Starting to disappear: The roof has come off Fred Truelove the turf accountants in 1965 as Victoria Square starts to make way for what was to be the site for the new Law Courts and police headquarters. In the distance, just behind the further dome of what was by now the Gaumont, is the new Huddersfield and Bradford (now Yorkshire) Building Society, in construction at the junction of Westgate and New John Street.

It isn't called Well Street for nothing. It was thought to be the site of the old Grammar School Well, from which the lower end of the town drew its water in the very old days. During reconstruction in 1961, the water supply became a nuisance and pumps were brought in, providing some casual amusement for people waiting for buses in Forster Square.

In the wet: the foundations for a support for the Dudley Hill underpass in Wakefield Road are flooded, causing problems for workers in 1968.

It took just two hours to winch the second span of this bridge over Wakefield Road during the widening scheme in 1967.
Six hours later it carried its first load – a truck full of railway ballast.

The first stretch of the widened Wakefield Road was almost ready for traffic here in 1968.

Down comes part of Union Street, in the city centre, in 1957 (above), and the massive redevelopment that was to change the whole face of the city was under way. The corner of O.S.Wain's can be seen to the right. In 1963 (right) the pile-drivers moved in.

Bathers bask in the August sunshine at the Lister Park Lido in 1973. It was opened in 1930 but, sadly, in 1973 cutbacks meant it opened only briefly. In 1982, £60,000 in repairs were needed. The following year it closed and it was razed to the ground in 1991.

Filled in and pulled down: The sad end of the Lister Park Lido after it had become a haven for drug addicts, vandals and dossers.

The boar's head on Bradford's coat of arms is there to recall the feat of Roger of Manningham, who is supposed to have killed a ferocious boar down by Bradford Beck in the middle ages. Apart from the arms, it is recalled here also in the cobbled Wild Boar Street. Wapping School is in the background.

Knockdown: One of the distinctive wooden cooling towers at Leather's Chemicals in Canal Road, a pungent part of the city, is pulled down during demolition of the works in 1972. It had been founded in 1750. Production shifted to St Helens.

Below: Pedestrians pick their way through a sea of mud in Darley Street and Kirkgate as Kirkgate Market was demolished in 1973. In the background is another vanished landmark, the hound which stood over the door of the Talbot Hotel.

Exterior of Lingards in Sunbridge Road shortly before its closure. Bargains, they said, were their business.

Last days at Lingards: The Bradford fabric shop, which had survived German bombing in the Second World War, finally closed its doors in 1977.

Visitors

Chapter Twelve

Royal smile: Queen Elizabeth the Queen Mother is applauded after attending a concert at St George's Hall in 1962. Afterwards she dined at City Hall.

Royal visit: King George V, partly shaded in the doorway, visits Lister's Mill during World War One.

Royal Limousine: Queen Elizabeth II makes her first visit to Bradford in October 1954. She had been crowned the year before.

Royal welcome: Bradford greets the Queen with an illuminated sign outside City Hall.

Queen Elizabeth and the Duke of Edinburgh on the steps of City Hall with Lord Mayor, Alderman Harry White, during her 1954 visit.

The Queen and Prince Philip are greeted by 20,000 schoolchildren as they drive around Park Avenue cricket ground.

Twenty years after: The Royal visit of November 1974 sees the Queen once again on the steps of City Hall with Lord Mayor Councillor Tom Hall, Chief Constable Ronald Gregory and Bradford's Chief Executive Gordon Moore.

The Queen goes on a Royal walkabout in The Tyrls during the 1974 Royal Visit.

The Prince of Wales, later George V, unveiled the statue of his grandmother, Queen Victoria, in 1904. It was during her
reign that Bradford had become a borough (1847) and a city (1897).

On the hustings: Labour Foreign Secretary George Brown supports the local candidates in the 1970 General Election. Bradford had four MPs in those days. Left to right are Norman Haseldine (Bradford West), Ben Ford (North), Edward Lyons (East) and Tom Torney (South).

Bradford-born Vic Feather (left), who became General Secretary of the TUC, is seen revisiting his roots for a BBC TV programme made to mark his retirement in 1973.

Sir John Barbirolli (left) conductor of the Halle Orchestra, and always a popular visitor, works on a score with
accompanist Rayson Whalley and soloist Paulina Stark at St George's Hall in 1969.

Field Marshall
Viscount
Montgomery of
Alamein is filmed
with the Little
Singers of Paris at St
George's Hall in
1954.

These 'Indians' let themselves down by getting drunk on the second night of their visit to Bradford in the 1920s. They got drunk and let the cat out of the bag – they were actually Cockneys, sworn to silence.

Always welcome: Father – and Mother – Christmas on their way to Busbys from Forster Square Station in 1936.

BBC TV reporter Fyfe Robertson, filmed outside City Hall in 1962 for the *Tonight* programme. He was making a film about the clock tower's carillon, now sadly silent.

Have a go! Popular broadcaster Wilfred Pickles is besieged by autograph hunters on a visit in 1954.

Then Prime Minister, Harold Wilson, brings up the rear on his way to be installed as Chancellor of the new Bradford University in November 1966. With him are vice-chancellor Dr E.G.Edwards and pro-chancellor Sir Charles Morris.

The Prime Minister confers an honorary degree on Bradford-born historian Alan Bullock, now Lord Bullock, Founding Master of St Catherine's College, Oxford.

Pint in hand, Conservative Party Leader Edward Heath meets the people in the Queen's Hotel, Bridge Street, Bradford, after addressing an eve-of-election meeting at St George's Hall in 1970. Two days later he was in Downing Street.

Defence Minister Denis Healey, old boy of Bradford Grammar School and Labour's 'intellectual bruiser', helps celebrate the first birthday of Thornton Labour Club in 1969.

By this time Chancellor of the Exchequer, Mr Healey entertains students and guests at St Joseph's College, Bradford in 1978.

Hemmed in: Zulfikar Ali Bhutto, founder of the Pakistan People's Party, addresses a rally on Infirmary Fields at the bottom of Lumb Lane in 1969. The rally was to have taken place in the Textile Hall, but there were too many people wanting to hear him speak.

Bhutto went on to become President of Pakistan and later Prime Minister. In 1978 he was sentenced to death on what his supporters felt was a trumped-up murder charge. His trial and subsequent execution in 1979 brought loud but peaceful demonstrations to the city.

The biggest literary event in the city in the 1950s was John Braine's novel *Room at the Top*. It soon attracted the attention of film-makers, and in 1958 cast, cameras and crews arrived to start filming. Director Jack Clayton (left), star Laurence Harvey, who was to play the ruthless Joe Lampton, and John Braine are seen here at the Victoria Hotel. Its proximity to the Exchange Station meant a bad few night's sleep for Harvey, who at one point rang the night porter and asked "can you tell me what time this hotel gets to King's Cross?"

Singer Tom Jones signs autographs for young admirers after performing at the Gaumont Cinema in 1968. A few years earlier he had seen his first hit, *It's Not Unusual*, hit the charts while appearing at the Lyceum Rainbow Club in the city.

Tom Courtenay (right), star of the film *Billy Liar*, made in and around Bradford in 1962, with a young man who was Anthony Bakes, and Courtenay's understudy for the role. Later, as Carl Gresham, he went on to success as showbiz agent and DJ.

Bradford-born England international footballer Albert Geldard returns to his old school, Whetley Hill, in 1974 and has a little heading practice with some of the pupils.

Comedian Les Dawson filming a sketch in Bradford Exchange Station in 1972. With him is actress Damaris Hayman.

Epic Hero: Film star Charlton Heston with young fans while visiting Bradford promoting his new film *The Greatest Show on Earth* in 1952. It was showing at the Odeon in Manchester Road.

Mary, the Princess Royal (left) arrives at Bradford Cathedral for the laying of the foundation stone of the new North Wing. On the right is the Bishop, Dr Alfred Blunt. Ironically he had been seen by some as instrumental in the abdication of the Princess' brother, Edward VIII.

...and Finally –
the T&A

Chapter Thirteen

Goldmine of information: the *T&A* Library, from which every picture in this book came, is an invaluable record in words and pictures of the city of Bradford, its history, its growth and its people.

This sad-looking football (left) was never a welcome sight to readers of the Yorkshire Sports, the *T&A's* Saturday 'Pink 'Un'. The gloomy face, incorporated in match reports, meant that Bradford City or Bradford Park Avenue had lost. On the other hand, (right), this was good news. The capering ball with a grin meant that City or Avenue had won. A draw was signalled by a rather neutral expression which suggested that one point was better than none.

Were the *T&A* to start a social club for youngsters today it would be highly unlikely to call it the Nignogs. Racism has put an unpleasant connotation on the term. However, in more innocent times, the Nignogs boasted as many as 40,000 members. At this 1933 revue at the Alhambra Theatre, one of many staged annually, the aeroplane bears the figure 30,000, which suggests that milestone had just been reached. The most famous Nignog Revue star was a lad from Leeds called Ernie Wiseman, later to become the half of Morecambe and Wise with the short, fat, hairy legs.

Apart from theatre, the Nignog club, founded in the late 1920s and running into the mid-1970s, boasted sections devoted to cycling – the bunch here are setting off for their weekly excursion in the mid-1960s – swimming (including formation) and its own football league. There was also a concert party which toured the West Riding giving shows which raised – as did the revue – thousands of pounds for local charities.

It pays to advertise, as this rear-entry West Yorkshire bus showed, standing at the Drake Street entrance to the *T&A* offices in the 1950s.

Probably the best news the *T&A* ever printed: the surrender of Germany on 7 May 1945. Winston Churchill takes pride of place below the other Allied leaders.

A world at their fingertips: It wasn't exactly the Internet, but the *T&A's* wireroom in 1968 was as up-to-the-minute as you could get at the time. Stories came in from Britain and the world at about the speed of a fast typist. Now they arrive electronically, faster than blinking.

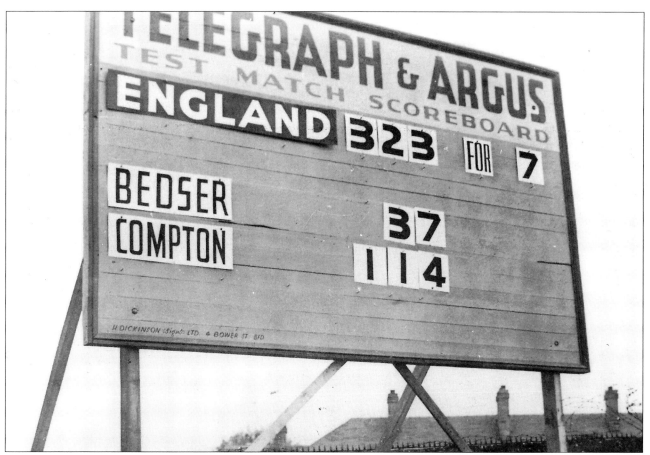

Keeping you in touch: the regularly updated scoreboard at Park Avenue which told Yorkshire fans how England were getting on in the Test Match. It was the days before transistor radios, and the days when Dennis Compton, champion of England and Brylcreem, was piling up the runs.

In the days before computers, the tools of a *T&A* sub-editor were simple: a pen or pencil, a pad of paper, a pot of glue and a ruler. Here, in 1967, *T&A* subs are hard at work on the Latest Special edition. The Last City is already on the desk.

Hot metal days: 'slugs' of type are assembled in a frame known as a 'chase' in the days before computerised typesetting arrived at the *T&A* in the 1970s. The *T&A* and its predecessor, the *Bradford Daily Telegraph*, were printed in this way for more than a century.

Printing plates go on the press in 1967. The lead alloy semi-cylinders were heavy and hot to handle. Modern plates, made of aluminium, are less than a millimetre thick.

This was always called 'the Santa Claus press' until it was replaced by the ones which now operate in the glass-sided Press Hall, opened in 1981. The name came from the manufacturers, who had emblazoned their name on the end of every reel-bar. It read 'Hoe, Hoe, Hoe, Hoe'.

The light, airy, and infinitely quieter Press Hall is opened in 1981 by the Duchess of Gloucester. She is seen here meeting the late Ken Oddy, then deputy editor of the *T&A*, who was widely admired throughout the community and his profession as a man who combined journalistic ability with principles and humanity.

Subscribers

Mr & Mrs Gordon & Joan Ackroyd
Maurice Ackroyd
Rowland L Ackroyd
Mrs Toni Kay Addlesee
A C Ainsworth
Mr A R Alderson
Florence Allan
John S Allison
Mrs Pauline F Allison
Leslie Ambler
Peggy Ambler
Stanley Keith Anthony
Mr Brian Appleyard
Colin Leslie Appleyard
Joan & Ernie Armitage
John R Armitage
William Kitson Asquith
Mr Eric Atkinson
Keith Atkinson
Glennis Attwood
Jean Auton
Mrs Margaret Avery
Mrs Maureen Axnix
Peter Timothy Aykroyd
Mr Brian Baines
Wm F Baines
Wm F Baines
Alan Bairstow
Walter Bairstow
Harry & Jennifer Baker
J M Bakes
Heather Baldwin
Stephen Ball
Bill Banks
Ray Banyard
Peter Baren
Cliff Barker
Mr E Barker
Leonard Barnes
Pauline L Barraclough
Eileen & Bryan Barratt
David Barrett
W L Barrett
Mr & Mrs J E Barthel
Francis Barton
Mrs Bessie Bassford & Mr Bill Bassford
Clifford Walter Bateson
Richard Anthony Bateson
Robert Bayles
Gordon Bayles
Timothy Shires Bean
C B Beaumont
Audrey & Bill Beck
Gerald Franklin Beevers
I Belcher
John Bennison
Mr C Benson
Dudley M Berry

Alan Keith Biggin
Lynn K Binner
C A Binns
Ernest Blackburn
Mr Clive Blackburn
Roy & Valerie Blackmore
D Blackwell
Eric Blades
Geoffrey Bland
Norman Bland
Harry Boardman
Mr Raymond C Bottomley
David Bould
J E Boulton
J & M Boxall
Albert E Bowtell
Terence Edward Bradbury
The Bradford Mechanics' Institute Library
J P Brady
Sheila Mary Bramley
K Brankin
Joyce Brian
David Brigg
Jack Wardman Briggs
Thomas Brock
Mr Eric Brocklehurst
Mr D R Brook
John Brook
Nicholas A Brook
Vera Priscilla Brook
Noreen L Brooke
Miss N Doreen Brookman
Miss N Doreen Brookman
Gladys E Broughton
Andrea Elizabeth Brown
Howard Micheal Brown
Geoffrey C Burn
Irene & Harry Burn
P Burnett
Joyce Burns
Mr S Burrell
Brian Burrows
Bernard Butterfield
Mrs Dorothy Bywater
John Bywater
Mr George Frederick Campbell
Keith Malcolm Carroll
George Donald & Joan Carter
Margaret C Carter
R S Carter
S M & J Cashman
Winifrid Caswell
E Chambers
M Chalcraft
Jeremy D Chantry
Alice A Chapman
Catherine Chapman
Leonard Chapman

Margaret Chapman
Richard Alan Chappell
Margaret C Charlton
C E & A Clark
Eric J Clark
Dr Colin G Clayton
Mr & Mrs D J Clayton
Mrs Sandra Mary Clayton
Harry Watson Clough
Derrick E Coates
Peter Coddington
Dr B W Cole
Mr Steven J Cole
B Collett
Mr Brian Connell
Barbara Connor
Mr E Conroy
J Trevor Constantine
John, Linda, Anthony & Matthew Cook
Alan Corbridge
Sheila Corby
M L & J Corina
Mr Ernest Corley
Eileen Cosgrove
Jean Costello
Mr Morton Cotterill
Keda Cowling
Mrs S I Cox
Mrs Sheila I Crabtree
Mrs Jean Craig
M L Crane
David Craven
Denise Craven
Eric Cresswell
Michael Crossland
Tony Cutts
Keith Dack
Mrs Janet Dalgliesh
Mr & Mrs K Dalton (now USA)
Kenneth Damman
Margaret Daniels
B Danylczuk
Mr Arthur Deacon
Robert W Denby
Denholme Conservative Club
Joan Dennison
B Denton
J P Dewhirst
Mrs Winifred Dewhirst
Ronnie Diaczenko
Brian Dickinson
Frank Dickinson
Keith Dickinson
Peter Dickenson
Keith Dinsdale
Kenneth Dinsdale
Mrs J A Dixon
K Dixon
Peter Djordjevic
Peter Dolby
R A Donkin
Ena Donnelly
Terence Dooling
Brian & Dorothy Douglas
Steven Paul Douglas
Stuart & Margaret Douglas

William Dowley
Alan Ward Drake
R H Draper
Mr John B Duff
Sheila Dunderdale
Carole & Clive Duprey
Peter Eastaugh
John C J Eaton
Agnes Egan
Father John Elders
Dr John Elliott
Stephen Elliott
Dorothy Ellis
Harry Ellis
Norman Ellis
Mrs Valerie O Ellis
Geoffrey Ellison
Geoffrey Ellison
Mrs L G Ellwood
Alma Elston
Gary Elston
Mrs J Elstrop
Eileen Emmett
Sandra Emmott
Ross A Epton
Michael Robert Epton
David Geoffrey Evans
John Brian Evans
Mrs Irene Everett
Mr Partick Farrington
S Richard Faulkner
E Fawbert
David Fenton
Irene Fielding
Philip Finder
Margaret Finn
David Firth
Evelyn Firth
Michael Firth
Joseph Foody, Esquire
George Ford
Malcolm F Foreman
J R Formby
Alice Foster
Fred W Foster
Mr Stanley Foster
Sheila Fox
Mr Raymond Franks, Lord of the Manor of
    Barwick-in-Elmet and of Thorner
Norman H Freeman
Terry Freeman
William Benedict Freeman
Mr Donald M French
Jean Furniss
Stanley Garnett
S & J Garnham
Bernard Garrod
Mr Frank Garrod
Mr & Mrs W Garside
Mrs V S Garthwaite
William & Hazel Gaunt
Kathleen Gibbons
Mrs Dorothy A Gibson
Malcolm & Glenys Gibson
G M & M Gidley
Mrs Joan Giles

Elsie Giles (née Pollard)
J M Gill
Frank Gilmore
The Gilroy Family
Mr Maurice Gledhill
H Glover
Mr Horace Gooderham
Douglas & Doreen Gooding
Walter Goodyear (formerly Malarkey)
Joan Mary Gott
R Goodison
Jean & John Gouldsbrough
Paul Goy
Sue & Jeff Grainger
Leslie Gray
G & S Grayson
Ray Greenhough
Gordon Greensmith
Mrs Adrienne Greenwood
David Paul Greenwood
Frank Wilfred Greenwood
Andrew John Gregory
Vincent Griffiths
Marian Grimshaw
Mrs Joan Gunn
Mrs Marjorie A Guy
Avice Haigh
Mrs Vera Hale
Betty Haley
Barrie & Linda Hall
Dorothy Hall
Graham Hall
Peter Hall
Peter & Valerie Hall
H D Hallett
Jean Hammond
John C Hammond
N Handley
Jonathan Charles Hannan
John Edward Hanson
Raymond Hanson
Stuart & Doreen Harding
Mrs Lallajean Hargreaves
Miss A Harland
Roland Harris
Mr Benjamin Harrison
Patricia Margaret Harrison
S Harriss & H Gower
Janette Hart (Douglas)
John David Hartley
John Haste
Miss Joyce Havers
Debbie Hawker
Frieda A Haworth
R Hazelwood
Mr E Hebdon
Renee Anne Hemingway
Corinne Frances Henderson
Alfred Stanley Heppleston
Anne Hepworth
Mrs K Elaine Hepworth
Irene Hewitt
Kenneth Joseph Hickey
Margaret Higgins
High Fernley First School
A Hill

Ida May Hill
Mrs Pamela J Hill
Ronnie Hill
William Hill
Pauline Janet Hillam
David Hird
John C Hird
Edna Hirst
Norman Hodgkins
D A Hodgson
Particia M Holland
Mr D Holmes
Geoffrey Holmes
Mr Raymond Holmes & Mrs Carol Holmes
Gordon Reginald Holroyd
Barry Holroyd
Mr Harry Stuart Hopwood
Matthew J Hornby
Mr Miles Horsley
Nancy Horsley
Kenneth Howe
J Huddleston
Mrs A Hudson
Alfred Hudson
Dorothy Hudson
Edith M Hudson
G A Hudson
Geoffrey Hudson
Kenneth Hudson
Mrs Isabel Hullah
Philip Hulme-Jones
R W & D M Hulson
Peter Hunt
Alma Maria Hunter
Mrs Lilian Hunter
Mr H Hutchinson
Mrs May Hutchinson
Mr Arthur Illingworth
Colin Illingworth
Carole A Inserra
Stanley Gordon Ives
Jennifer Jackson
Mr Joseph Jackson
Edward Jagger
Frederick Trevor Kellett Jagger
Mrs Dorothy Jeffrey
Herbert Johnson
Herbert Johnson
Walter Johnson
Mrs Hilary Jones
Mrs Ruth Mary Jones
Stanley Kay
Laurence Kearns
Mr Sean Keating
A Keighley
T A Keighley
Jack H Kell
Marjorie Kelly
Josephine Kenny
Gary Kenzie
Jean Kershaw
Stephen Kershaw
Mrs Dorothy Kilbank
P A Killeen
D M King
Mrs K Kingswell

S Kirk
Mr G & Mrs R M Kirton
Alan Kirwan
Robin Kitson
Robin Kitson
Betty Knapton
Edgar & Vera Knapton
Geoffrey F Knight
Mr John W Knopwood
Mrs M Knowles
Mr & Mrs R J Lacey
James Michael Laffey
Michael Lamb
Mrs D Larner
Albert & Jane Lawrence & Family
Marc Lawrence
Sydney Lawrence
B Lawson
George Lawton
Sheila M Lawton
Mr Jack Layton
Dorothy Ledgard
Richard Lee-Van Den Daele
Mrs Gladys Leece
Mrs A Lees
Margaret Patricia Spencer Leng
Betty Leonard
John Leonard
Mrs K Lightowlers
Dr & Mrs P A Linley
Mr Frank Lister
Robert Lister
Gordon Lockwood
Mrs J M Long
Mrs Lynn Lovatt
Mr James Lovett
Jill Ludbrook
Norman Lusher
Muriel & Peter McAndrew
Mrs M McCabe
R J McCabe
Gerald McCauley
G Mace
Ian McGregor
Mr & Mrs M J M Mackay
Annie & Leonard Mackinder
A J McKinnon-Waters
Frances McLachlan
Barbara Maden
Daniel Joseph Magee
Hazel Magill
A B Mahoney
David Mallinder
Mrs Ann Mallinson
Janice Maloney
David C Malt
Richard J Malt
Barbara Manojlovic
Richard Marcisz
Mr & Mrs D J Marsden
Derek Marsden
Albert Marshall
D Mason
William Mason
Mr David Lloyd Matthews
Sidney Matthews

Brian Mawson
Miss Leila Mead
Mr Fred Medley
Colin Mellor
Christopher John Melvin
Peter Meredith
Harry Metcalfe
Walter Metcalfe
David Miller
Mr Keith Mills
Shirley Milner
Mr & Mrs C G R Milnes
Mrs Doreen Mintoft
Brian Ian Mitchell
Mr Harry Mitchell
Albert William Moore
David Stuart Morris
Mr Joseph Mortimer
Eric & Christine M Moulson
Raymond N Muff
David Mullinder
Mr Albert Murgatroyd
Jonathan Murgatroyd
A M Murphy
Mr K J Murphy
Alan & Diane Murray
David & Janet Muschamp
Jack Ingham Myers
Miss V M Nathan
Shirley M Naylor
Francis G Naylor
Mr M Neilan
Reg Nelson
Sandra J Newborn (née Tempest)
New Hey Road Methodist Church
Mrs Hannah Newton
Nigel R Newton
John M Nilen
F R A Nixon
Joseph O'Connor
J & S J Oldfield
Ian G Oliver
Miss Florence Osborn
Barry Oxtoby
Len Padgett
Mrs Muriel Palmer
Mr N Papworth
Mr N Papworth
Mr N Papworth
Ralph Parish
Carole Parker
K & C Parker
Norman Parker
Bernard Parry
David Patefield
Gerald Patterson
Mr Charles Richard Pawson
Douglas & Shirley Pawson
Eric Pearson
Ellen & Trevor Pearson
Richard Pearson
Roy & Betty Pearson
Mr M Peel
Michael Pendleton
Rod Pennell
Jack Pennington

Mr & Mrs N R Perrins
Derek Pickles
John Pickles
J T Pickles
M Pickles & R Pickles
Miss M Pickles
Brian & Glenda Pickford
Mrs Alice Picton
Mr Jack Pitt
A D Pollard
Mr J G Prentice
Mr Derek Priestley
Mrs Eunice E Purcell
Betty Puttick
Alan George Quick
Doreen Quick
Norman Rainbow
Roland Ransom
Mr John Rawnsley
John Rawnsley
Mrs E Rayner
Mr Graham Reeday
Graham T Reid
Michael Reid
Cecil J R Rhodes
R A & C P Rhodes
B Richardson
C & M Richardson
K D Richardson
Anne Patricia Riches
Pierre A Richterich
Pierre A Richterich
Pierre A Richterich
Pierre A Richterich
Pierre A Richterich
V S Riles
Brendan Riley
William Roach
Betty Roast
Doreen Robertshaw
Malcolm Robertshaw
Mrs Shirley Robertson
Bill Robinson (Yeadon)
Mr David Robinson
Derek Robinson
Ivor Robinson
Jack Robinson
Mr & Mrs Philip W Robinson
R Robinson
Mr A A Rodgers
John Roman
Mr Stuart D Rose
Sheila Diane Christine Royle
David M Royston
Graham & Margaret Rushforth
Trevor Rushforth
Susan Rushworth
Kevin Rylatt
M P Sattenstall
A Saxton
John Saxton (Williamstown, Australia)
Ian Gordon Schofield
Fred Scott
Valerie & Allen Sefton
Mrs May Sellers
Peter Shackleton

Pauline Shackleton
Denis Sharkey
Mrs E Sharp
Mr & Mrs J Sharp
Tony & Margaret Shaw
Pamela Mary Shaw
David Shearing
Brian & Norma Shillaker
Dennis Shutt
Mrs Sheila Sidney
Mrs Sheila Sidney
Anthony Silson
Mary P Silson
Roy Simcock
Stanley & Joan Sinfield
Leslie Skelly
Andrew Elliott Smith
Bernard Smith
Miss C T Smith
Claire L Smith
Mr David I Smith
Iain G Smith
Iain G Smith
John G Smith
Peter Roy Smith
Raymond Smith
Ronald Scott Smith
Sydney F Smith
David & Mollie Somerville
Clarice Roseline Spencer
Mrs S Spencer
Mrs Squire
Paul Staincliffe
Simon Andrew Stainsby
Peter Stanley
Ian Stansfield
Susannah Stansfield
Clare Staunton
Mrs Elizabeth Starkey
Fred Stephenson
Marjorie I Stephenson
Mrs James B Stott
Mr Eric Suggitt
Roy Summers
D W Surman
Albert & Mollie Sutcliffe
K & A E Sutcliffe
Colin L Sutton
Sylvia Sweet
Mr D Swift
Nicholas Tagg
Denis Talbot
T Tate
Albert Howard Taylor
Anne & Geoffrey Taylor
Mrs Maureen Teale
Brian J Tempest
C V Tempest
Mrs Elaine G Tetley
Jack Tetley
Alan Thackray
Alan Thompson
Edward Thompson
Magdaline Thompson
Margaret Thompson
Philip Thompson

G H Thomson
John S Thornton
Mrs Jean Tighe
David Barry Tillotson
Stephen Tillotson
M E Toft
Darren Tordoff
Mr David A Tordoff
Jack Turner
G & M Twentyman
Enid Vale
Mr & Mrs J G Waddington
Mary Waddington
Mr John Wadsworth
Alexander Walker
The Walker Family of Bradford Moor
M Walker
Peter D Walker
Mary Wallace
Desmond A Walsh
Geoffrey Walshe
Doreen Walter
Adrian Ward
Frances Ward
Malcolm & Eve Ward
Joan E Wardman
Mrs Gladys Waterhouse
L Watkins
Mrs Patricia Watson
Richard Watson
Bob Watson
Eric Watterson
Eric Watterson
Michelle M Webb
Michael Welch
Thomas E Wellings
Mrs Edith Grace Wells
Anthony L West
P R West
Terence Edgar Wetherell
Mrs N Whalley
Mr Clifford Wharton
James Whelan
Amy Whitaker
Mrs Julie Whitaker
Arthur Whitehead
K T Whitehead
Neil Stuart Whitfield
Mr Leslie Whitehead
Clare & Benjamin Whitham
Duncan Whitley
Jack Widdop
Brian Wilkinson
Mrs B Wilkinson
Mr Brian A Wilkinson
Colin Wilkinson
David Wilkinson
Mr D Wilkinson
John Wilkinson
Mary Alice Wilkinson
James Wilks
J A Willcox
James S Williams
James Derek Willis
Philip Simon Willis
Gordon & Avril Wills

Julian Gawain Clifford Wills
Mathew & Kathryn Wills
Mr Andrew R Wilson
Donald Eric Wilson
Edna Wilson
Eric Wilson
Geoffrey Wilson
Mr John Wilson
Joseph Barker Wilson
Mary H Wilson
Mr & Mrs J J Winder
Mrs K A Winder
R J Winterbourne
David Winterton
Mr Dennis Wood
K L Wood
L Wood
Leslie Wood
Richard F Wood
Roy Wood
Paul Andrew Woodcock
Donald & Ivy Woodhead
Mrs Ellen Woodrow
Elizabeth Mary Woods
Peter Woodward
Douglas L Woolner BEM
Arthur Worley
Arthur Calvert Wormald
David Wormald
Charlotte E Wright
Peter Anthony Wright
Mr Tom Wright
Mrs Mary Yates
John Yearsley
Malcom Yearsley
Ronald Byron Yearsley
Jack & Norma Yorke
Pauline Young